See & Draw Like An Artist

See & Draw Like An Artist

A Practical Self-Paced Guide for Adults To Learn Drawing Skills Quickly

Written and illustrated by

V. L. MOORE

Book design by V. L. Moore
Cover design by V. L. Moore

First Edition: November 2024

ISBN: 9798345831076

For Cristine; I love the way you draw horses…and friends.

Contents

Acknowledgements

Thank you, Rick, Sue, and Leenie for supporting me during this whole process. I could not have managed this without you.

Also, thanks to my friend Peggy for her patience in making me understand those printing details that I need to know, even though I was not especially interested at the time. I'm a lucky woman and love you all.

Introduction

Welcome to the captivating world of drawing, where lines on paper become windows of imagination, expression, and creativity. Whether you're an absolute beginner or looking to refine your skills, this journey into the art of drawing is an invitation to unlock the boundless possibilities of self-expression and learning to "see" like an artist.

I grew up on the lower Potomac River where it meets the Chesapeake Bay and spent my childhood running in the woods, along the little beach, or floating on the nearby pond. Each day I would sketch some of the wonders that I discovered. When I had no paper, I would draw on anything, such as rocks, wood, walls, or even cabinets – much to my mom's dismay. I've been drawing ever since I could hold a pencil in my tiny hand. When I was very small, around three or four, I developed a passion for horses.

It's the first of my many obsessions. I would ask everyone I saw to draw a horse for me and was never satisfied with the pictures that others would draw. Finally, in exasperation, my mom said; "Well, draw it yourself!" So I did, sparking the beginning of my second obsession, drawing.

Dedication

This book is dedicated to everyone who dreams of living in the moment and taking a little time to peer into that moment and appreciate it, providing access to your creativity. That singular moment will never exist again.

To all those who linger in that moment, looking deep and wanting to capture it, in order to share with others their own creative vision, I salute you.

Those are the people with the soul of an artist.
Those people are geniuses.
Those people are you.

Chapter 1: Getting Started

In this book, we will delve into the basics of still life and landscape drawing. I will encourage you to work from life, meaning that you draw things that actually exist in front of you. For example, I may ask you to draw a cup, a bird or a tree. I also may ask you to draw from a photograph. Never fear. I'll offer simple tasks, methods and tips that will help you find success whether you are an absolute beginner or someone wanting to kick it up a notch.

I believe that you can draw like an artist. You just need to have two things -- the desire and the skillset. Since you have my book then you obviously have the desire. So, in the pages that follow I will provide you with a skillset and teach you to see like an artist!

Remember, in art there are no mistakes, only opportunities to learn and grow. This book is not just about creating beautiful drawings; it's about nurturing a creative mindset, embracing the process, and discovering the unique artist that resides within you.

Embrace Your Creative Journey

The idea of picking up a pencil and sketching may seem daunting, but fear not. This book is designed to be your guide, offering a structured approach to the fundamentals of drawing. From understanding lines and shapes to exploring light, shadow, value, and perspective, we will embark on a step-by-step exploration of artistic foundations.

Before we dive in, let's get familiar with the basic tools and materials that will accompany you on this creative journey. Whether it's the tactile feel of a pencil, the clean canvas of a sketchbook, or the myriad possibilities of erasers and shading tools, let's get your artistic toolkit ready.

Clear your mind and let's embark on this exciting adventure. Whether you're sketching for relaxation, self-expression, or to refine your skills, each stroke is a step closer to unlocking the artist within.

Workspace

Many prefer to create an inviting yet not necessarily organized workspace for an enjoyable drawing experience. Keep your tools within reach and consider adding personal touches that inspire creativity.

Most artists prefer working in a room with north facing windows because it provides ambient light without harsh hotspots and shadows. The area should be well lit with a comfortable chair and a spacious surface for your sketchbook or paper. If you use a light, place it opposite the hand you draw with so that you don't create hand shadows while you work.

Your workspace can be anywhere. A coffee shop, subway, waiting room, beach, or park bench all are great places for sketching. As long as you can access your tools, that's all that matters.

Materials & Tools

With anything you do, it is important to have the right tools for the job. Let's start with a fun fact. The right tool is NOT the Number 2 pencil you were required to have in school!

Pencils

Different drawing **pencils** offer various shades. HB pencils are medium. Mechanical pencils with HB lead in sizes .5 and .3 are useful for doing measurement lines and fine uniform lines or for hair or hard edges, like buildings.

Graphite "B" pencils have blacker or darker graphite and are for the artist with a softer touch. The "H" pencils are harder, using lighter-weight graphite and are more suitable for artists with a heavy hand. Whether they are H or B pencils, they come in a range of numbers from 1-9.

B9 pencils are the darkest and B2 are lighter. The changes in tone are subtle, so don't assume that scribbling harder on the paper will make it darker. You'll just ruin your paper and get hand cramps. You don't want arthritis or carpel tunnel symptoms because of your grip.

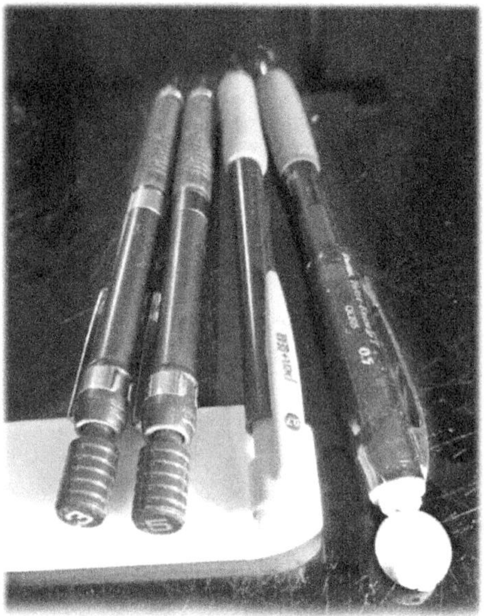

Mechanical Pencils

Artist Pencils

Over time you will learn which pencils or combination of pencils will work best for you.

Tip: As you draw, try to develop a lighter hand and a loose grip to reduce stress on your bones and tendons.

Smudge Sticks

Smudge sticks are the only choice for natural and realistic shading. This is the best little drawing accessory kit. It comes with a soft white and a kneadable eraser, a good assortment of smudge sticks, a sharpener, and a sand pad for honing the point of your pencils between sharpening. I highly recommend getting something like this: the Master's Touch Drawing Kit!

Eraser

A good eraser is your ally in correcting mistakes and refining details. Consider having a **kneadable eraser** for versatility. Kneadable erasers are very soft and pliable and are highly unlikely to damage your paper.

I prefer to use a **soft white eraser**, which comes in a variety of shapes and sizes. The important thing about the white erasers is that they also don't damage your paper. Colored erasers like the pink or green ones that folks buy for kids in school are hard erasers. They may be convenient, fitting on top of those Number 2 school pencils, but make no mistake, they will damage your paper and your hard work. I make a point to carry my white eraser everywhere, but like to have a kneadable, as well.

Tip: Avoid using pink or other colored erasers. The colored erasers are hard and will damage your paper.

Eraser Shield

An Eraser Shield is a must for high detail work. What is it? It's a magical device that allows you to make small corrections without having to redo a large portion of your drawing. Your shield will make you feel like an artistic superhero!

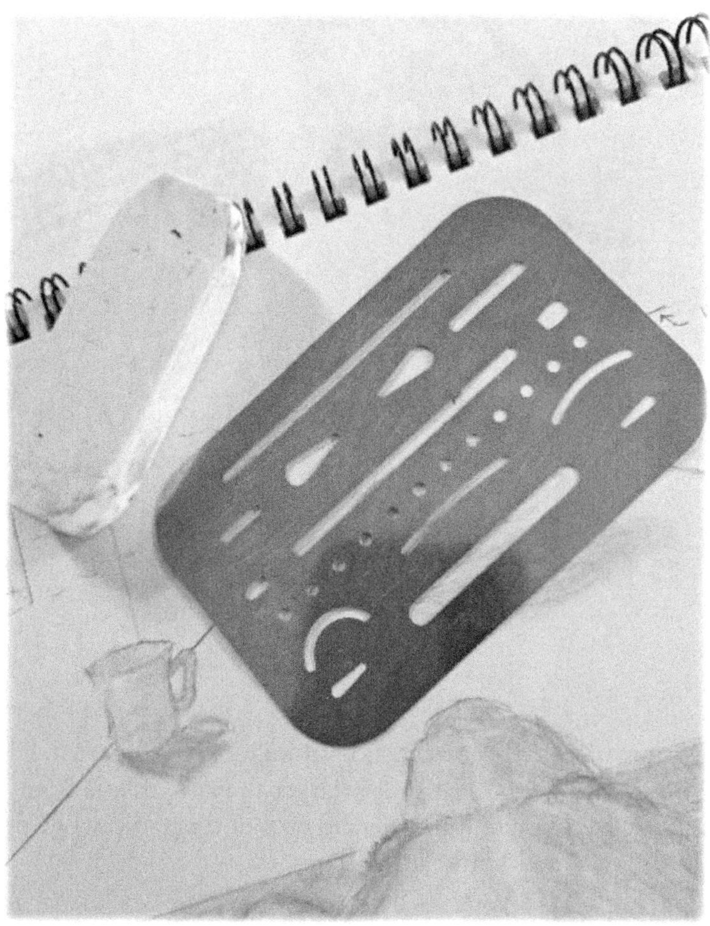

Sketchbooks

Choose **Sketchbooks** with quality paper that suits your preferences. Spiral-bound sketchbooks are convenient for lying flat while drawing. I like smoother paper that is 60-pound to 90-pound weight. The lighter weight is good for using with a light table. A light table allows you to trace portions of imagery. Below are assortments of small sketchbooks and larger spiral-bound sketchpads.

For most "art pieces" I recommend a 9-inch by 12-inch pad. This size allows you to create a good 8x10 or larger drawing that is both frame-worthy and big enough that fingers and eyes don't cramp while trying to cram a lot of value work into a tiny space.

Tip: Get a smaller sketch journal (5x7 or 6x9) to use for honing your skillset.
Practice! Practice! Practice!

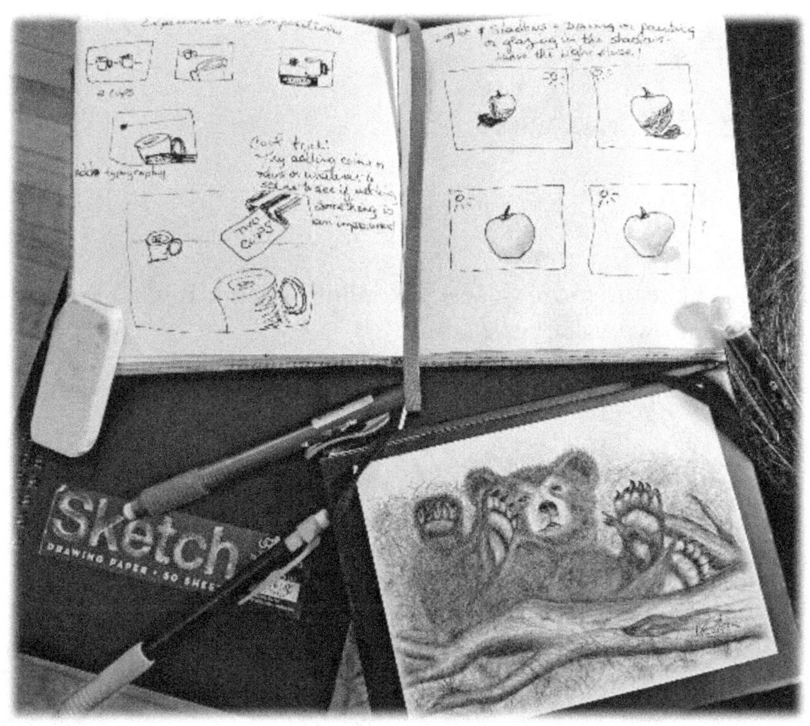

Most Important Tool – **Value Scale**

A value scale allows artists to define and organize different shades of light and dark and all shades of gray in between. In artist terminology, *value* refers to the lightness or darkness of the highlights and shadows.

Tonal values are depicted in grayscale from dark (black) to light (white).

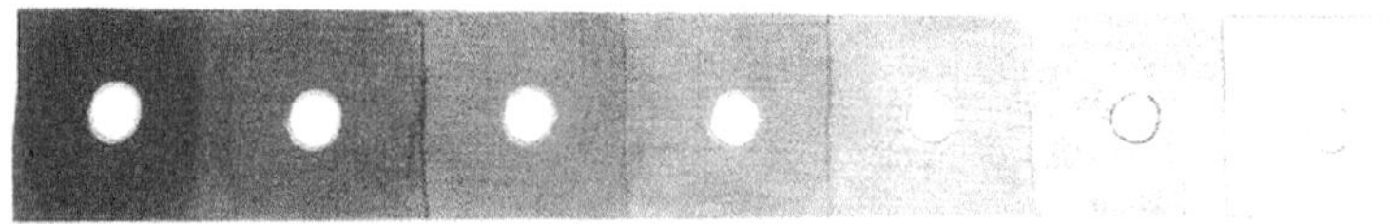

Value scale

You can get a ready-made value scale online or in any reputable art store or make your own value scale (above).

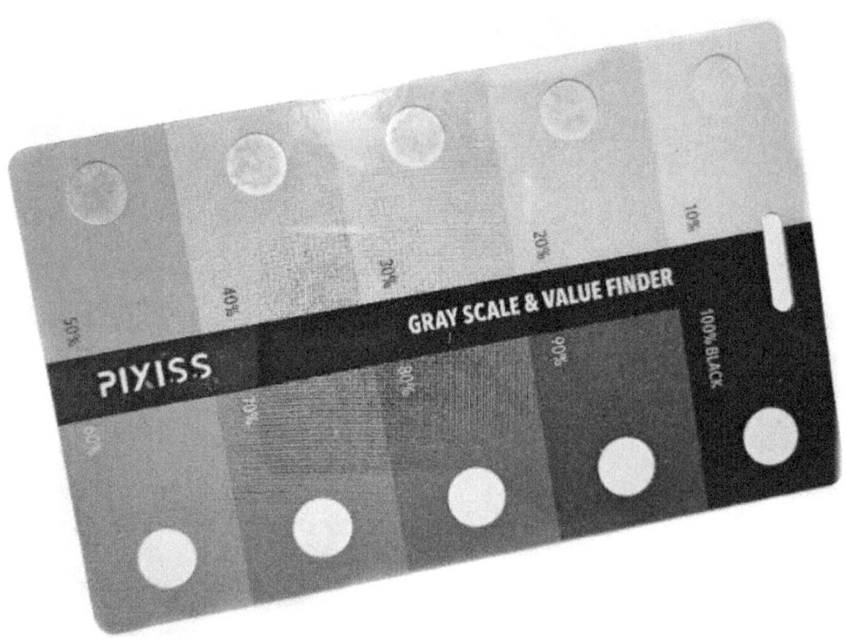

Other Important Tools!

Your **cell phone** is the other most important tool to help you on your journey to develop an artistic eye. Use it for reference photos of what you're drawing. Removing the color from a scene is the easiest way to evaluate values and tones according to brightness. You can do that by snapping a photo and then editing the picture to remove all color. Save a black-and-white copy. You will see the various values of each color in your image. This is how you learn the value of color. It also helps you learn to see how to translate a three-dimensional scene into something two-dimensional on a flat screen. Don't leave home without your phone!

Pencil Sharpener

It's important to keep your pencils sharp, which adds precision to your work as well as maximum surface use area for shading. You should have at least a couple of sharpeners; I have an electric one on my desk. It's not required though. The small portable ones are great and all you really need.

Drawing is not an expensive hobby. You can get started with only the things I have suggested here for a very small investment. However, there are a few other things I would like to suggest. Why? Because the one with the coolest tools generally wins. Especially if they use them!

Strongly suggested items

Here are a few optional but highly recommended items. Get a cotton or nylon **Fabric Glove** for your drawing hand. Please, no MJ jokes. I use the glove for where my hand rests on the paper while working. You can use a scrap piece of paper instead, but the glove is cool. I cut the tips off of the first three fingers because I like to feel my pencil in hand.

If you don't have a cotton glove then I suggest a **soft 1-inch paint brush,** a **drafting brush,** or a piece of **cotton fabric** (like a glove). This is useful for sweeping across your paper to remove eraser crumbs and helping to keep those grubby paws off the paper. I like a drafting brush when sitting at my desk, but it's big and unwieldy for travel, which is why I choose a fluffy paint brush or just use my gloved hand.

Finally, get a **bag or case** to hold your things. Some artists are organized and prefer Franklin Planner-style kits. Others like a simple pencil case or art bag that they can toss into a backpack.

Gloves, soft brush, pencil case/bag kit

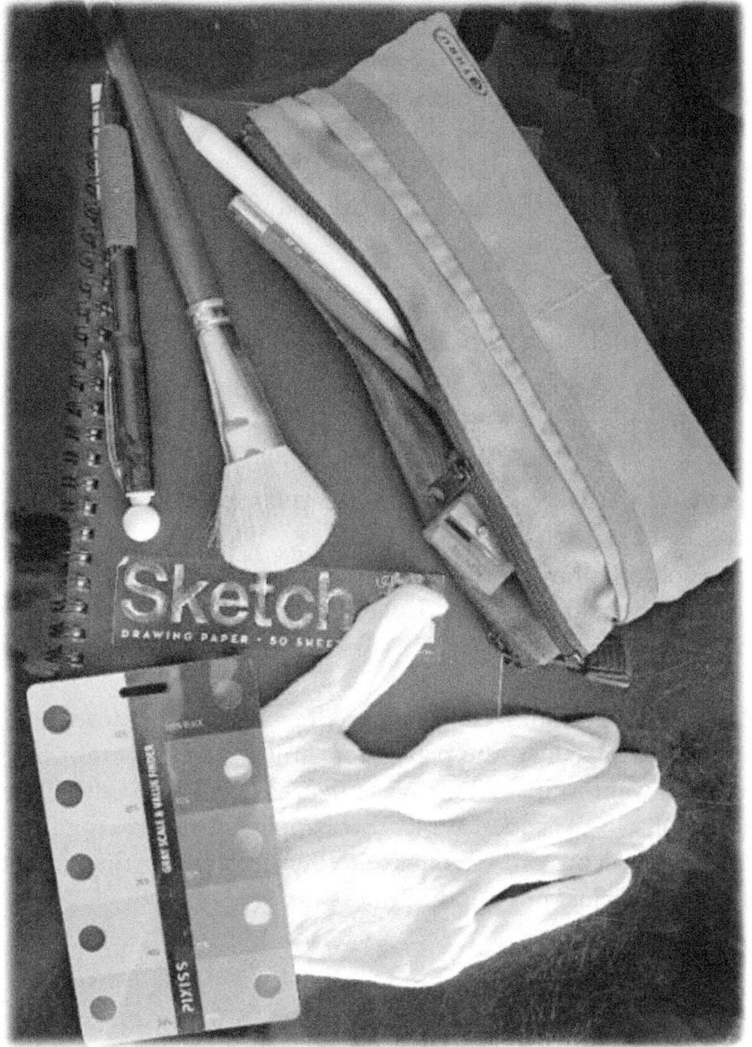

Whatever works for you is perfect and that's all you need!

Hone Your Craft!

In order to hone your craft, I recommend that you also use the smaller sketchbook or sketch journal and carry it with you always. Sketch journals are usually 5x7 or 6x9 booklets with unlined paper. They often are used by artists while they are sitting in waiting rooms, riding buses or subways, hanging out in parks or coffee shops, or anywhere you can stop for a few moments and sketch a scene. As with any skill, practice makes perfect. If you start sketching daily you will see significant improvement in your skill level pretty quickly. It's a valuable habit to get into.

One More Thing: The Rule That Shall Not Be Broken!

There really is only one rule that should be adhered to when working with pencil and paper. This rule is:

Keep your grubby hands off the paper!

Never touch the drawing surface of your paper with your bare hand or fingers. Fingers add oil to the paper, which turns the paper yellow and makes it impossible to erase.

The last thing you want to do is start a drawing over because the oils in your hands have stained the paper. It's a mistake that cannot be fixed. No one will want to buy an art piece that has yellowish oily skin stains or eraser holes in the paper. When that happens, you have doubled your time and work. You also have halved your income for the project as a result, and that's just not good business.

Notice the scrap paper (paper towel) beneath my hand. If you don't have a glove, use scrap paper!

Tip: Avoid using your finger to create shadows or shade, which will stain you paper. Use a smudge stick instead.

Drawing Lines

Lines are the building blocks of your drawings, each with its own character and purpose. Drawing straight lines horizontally, vertically, and diagonally improves your control and precision. Drawing smooth, flowing curves is crucial for creating organic shapes and capturing fluidity in your work. Variable line lengths add dynamism to your work.

Exercise 1

Before diving into drawing, familiarize yourself with all of your tools and supplies. Sharpen your pencils. Check out the difference in lines that each makes. Note the difference when using a mechanical pencil, which is held upright, as opposed to a B6 pencil. Take time to examine and see the tones that each of your pencils creates.

Practice holding your pencil comfortably. Experiment with different grips to find what feels natural for you. The blank page can be intimidating but remember that every artist starts somewhere. Embrace the freedom to create and let go of perfectionism. Play with each pencil.

A. Start by making simple marks on your paper. Experiment with different types of lines -- straight, curved, thick, thin, short, and long. Hold the mechanical pencil upright, practice drawing lines and parallel lines.

Try holding each of your other pencils upright and sideways, making thin lines and broad strokes. Do this with all your pencils. Notice the different tonal quality of each pencil. Get in the habit of keeping your pencils sharp and ready to sketch. This exercise helps you get comfortable with your tools and builds muscle memory.

Remember to place scrap paper between your hand and the drawing paper or use your glove.

Practice good habits from the start!

B. Draw parallel lines that start close together at the top but get farther apart at the bottom so that it looks kind of like a triangle, but without the lines touching. Next, draw horizontal lines across the parallel lines th are close together at the top and get farther apart at the bottom.

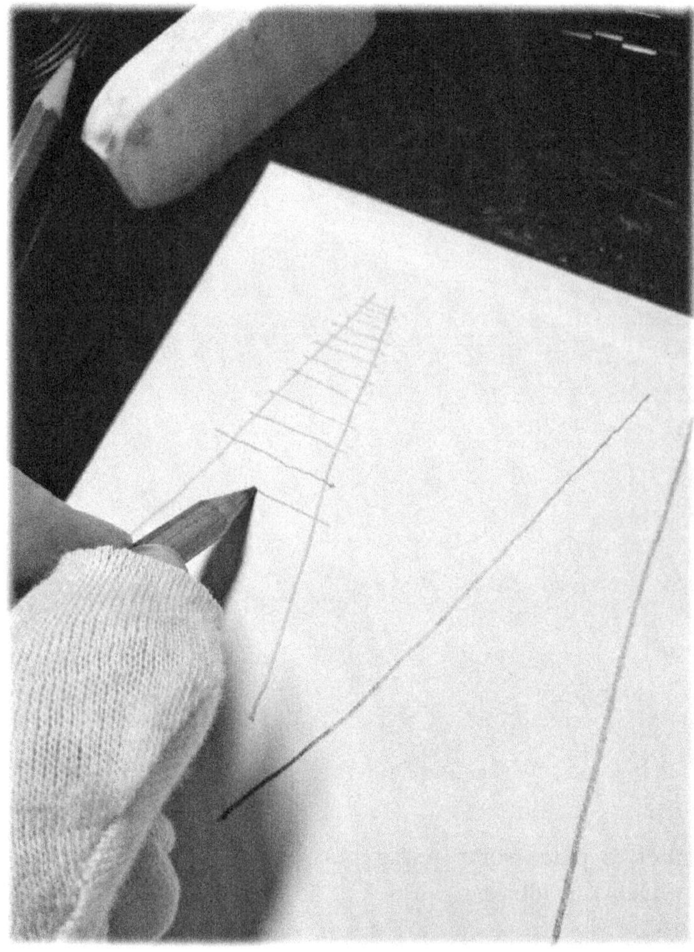

Look at the lines on the right. Can you imagine something in a landscape that might look like this? Maybe a road?

Now look at the lines on the left. Does it look like a ladder or railroad tracks? These questions should help you "see" the way an artist sees things. This is a little abstract, but it still should look sort of like railroad tracks leading toward the horizon. Things look smaller as they get farther away and near the horizon.

A. Draw "S" curves using at least three different pencils. Try drawing some with pencils upright and some with your pencils sideways. Use your smudge sticks to blur your lines, or create new lines with the smudge sticks.

Draw parallel "S" curves, where they are close together at the top and gradually get further apart at the bottom. Do this several times using different pencils.

What could these lines look like to you? Could they be the beginning of an artist trying to draw a river or…?

Can you see how those parallel lines could be the beginning stages of an artist drawing a road?

B. Write down in your sketchbook journal, what do you hope to achieve through drawing? Whether it's relaxation, self-expression, or skill development, setting intentions helps guide your practice and keeps you motivated. Jot down your goals and we will revisit this later.

Consider these first strokes as the first step in your artistic journey. You are learning to "see" like an artist! There's nothing better than looking back to where you started and seeing the results of how far and well you have progressed.

Conclusion

Congratulations! You have accomplished your first step in this journey toward creative expression. You've learned to use some of your important tools, specific artist language, and skills to practice as you embark on this journey. Remember that each stroke is a step toward improvement. Enjoy the process and let your creativity flow freely. In the chapters ahead, we'll delve deeper into the fundamentals of drawing, building on the foundation you've laid in this Getting Started section. Happy drawing.

Chapter 2: Understanding Two Dimensions

Now that you've set up your creative space and familiarized yourself with some of your drawing tools, it's time to delve into some more foundational elements of drawing. When drawing, you are working in a two-dimensional (2-D) medium. That medium is the flat page that has height and width.

Lines & Shapes & Forms: Oh My!

You've already started to explore the versatility of **Lines**. Now you're going to delve into the significance of different types of **Shapes**, and how mastering basic **Forms** will be the cornerstone of your drawing skills. All **Shapes** are created by single lines. A triangle can be created by one line connected at three corners. You never have to pick up your pencil from the paper to create a **Shape**. Similarly, a square or rectangle is created by one line connected at four corners. A circle has no corners at all but is still one continuous line. Understanding these **Shapes** lays the groundwork for constructing object **Forms**.

Notice that the basic **Shape** of a cone is two shapes in one. It's a triangle and a circle used together to create a rudimentary cone, which is a **Form**. A **Form** is created by combining multiple shapes that create an object that exists in three dimensions and is represented below in two dimensions. Below are the primary 2-Dimensional (2-D) shapes used to create Forms:

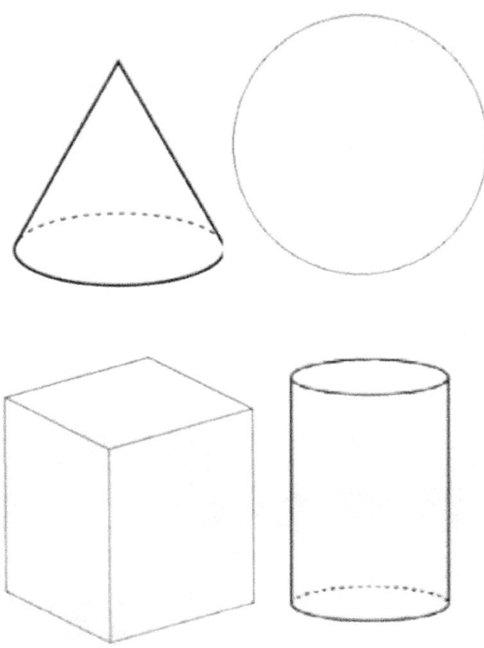

Triangle and Circle = Form of a Cone.

The circle is one line, no corners and is always a shape. A form of a Ball can be created only by adding light and shadow.

Three Squares = Form of a Block or Cube.

A Rectangle or Square and two Circles on the ends = Form of a Tube

These are the basic shapes and forms used to create any image on paper.

These images are never going to win any artistic awards, right? However, these are the basic shapes and forms of everything in our reality! They are sometimes called *symbols* because they are used to represent or communicate more complex images and thoughts. Most symbols are two-dimensional (2-D). Every shape or symbol of anything in our reality can be boiled down to a combination of **Lines** and these four **Shapes/Forms**.

I can hear your eyes rolling around your head right now. I'm serious! Okay let's test my theory. What about a teardrop? A teardrop looks like a cone and a circle. Flip it upside down and you have an ice cream cone.

What about hearts? I would say that's nothing more than two circles overlapping with an inverted cone. What if you look down at the heart from above? Wouldn't it look like a big butt ready to twerk? What if you add dots to the center of each of the circles in the heart shape? Could it then remind someone of a womans chest?

You can't unsee that now, right? That, my friend, is an example of learning to "see" like an artist. Sometimes, hormones play a role in seeing and sex definitely sells in the world of art.

Okay, how about a tree? Yeah … that too! A pine tree would be a tube and a cone or several cones on top, but an oak would be a tube and a circle or several smaller circles overlapping.

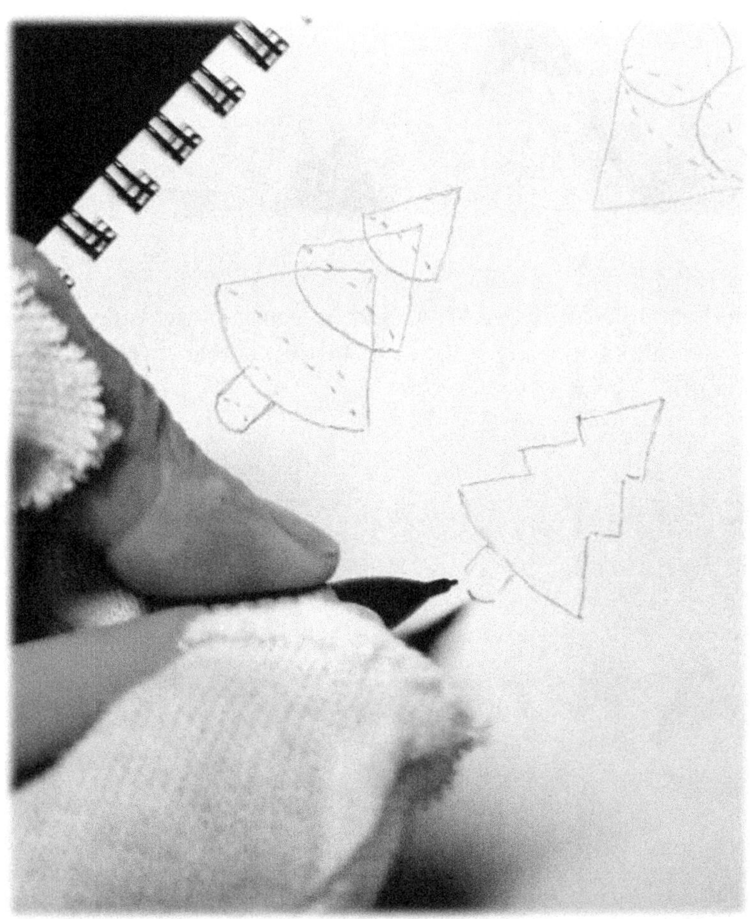

Another example of my theory would be every word you've ever read. Text is just marks on a page (lines and shapes) that are symbols of words and thoughts.

Tip: Remember to use your glove or scrap paper under your hand to keep the paper clean. Get used to using ALL of your tools and develop good habits!

Exercise 2: Lines & Shapes & Forms. Oh My!

As you work through these exercises, embrace the freedom to experiment and make mistakes. Remember, each stroke brings you one step closer to honing your drawing skills.

A. Combine lines, shapes, and forms to create simple drawings. Start with basic objects such as the teardrop, ice cream cone, or heart. Gradually introduce more complex forms.

B. Use each of the four basic shape-forms in the objects that you draw. Play with them! For example: Draw a book. Then try drawing an open book. This may seem tricky but it's not really. Here's a hint. Turn your teardrop sideways and draw an elongated square (also known as a rectangle) below that overlaps your teardrop. Then flip it. See image below.

C. Finally, create a simple bird. The beak is a cone. It can have a block head or a circle head. Eyes always start as circles. The body could be a circle, triangle, or tube or a cube. This is exactly how many cartoonists create their characters.

Use a variety of combinations of shapes to create birds. The tail could be one cone or several. Legs can be tube shapes or simple lines. Use your own imagination and create something fun!

Conclusion

This practical application reinforces the concepts you've just learned and encourages you to use your tools. I always found it odd when an artist would say, "I can't draw that!" Once you figure out that everything in reality is just a collection of lines and those four shapes/forms, you have discovered the big secret. Then, with a little practice looking at things this way and seeing those things the way an artist sees them, you can draw anything. Boom! Now you're an artist and magician. It's time to create some magic!

Chapter 3: Creating Three-Dimensions By Adding Value

When we draw lines and shapes, our pencils do not create a visible depth. But we do create the illusion of depth, the third dimension (3-D). How? I've already told you. Artists are magicians!

Now you are ready to learn how to create the real magic of a **Three-Dimensional (3-D)** image on a **Two-Dimensional (2-D)** surface. The magic is created with light and shadow and is the secret sauce for creating the illusion of 3-D. Light and shadow are the artists' tools for creating depth, form, and mood in drawings.

In this chapter, we'll explore fundamental concepts of light and shadow, techniques for shading, and ways to bring your drawings to **3-D** life through the interplay of illumination and darkness.
Remember those shapes we talked about before? They were a Circle, a Triangle, a Square, and a Rectangle. Look what happens when you add a bit of light and shade? The world shifts!

The circle shape becomes a ball form.

The triangle shape becomes a cone form.

The square shape becomes a block form.

The circle/rectangle shape becomes a tube form.

Balls, cones, blocks, and tubes are what artists use to represent 3-dimensional objects on a 2-dimensional page. These corresponding 3-D forms create everything in our reality. I'm serious! Everything can be drawn with lines and these four forms shown above. You are learning to see them as the artist sees.

Value

The interplay between light and shadow creates a range of **values**, from the darkest darks to the lightest lights. Experimenting with different pencils and shading techniques to capture this tonal range will add depth and realism to your drawings. Let's delve into the concept of value.

First of all, the importance of **value** cannot be overstressed in your work, and we are not talking about monetary value either! Although, it never hurts to keep that in mind, I'm not focusing on that aspect of art in this context. When someone says a work is high or low value, they are referring to the overall contrast of the piece.

High Contrast value means there are bright whites, strong crisp light and deep darks, referring to shadow in an art piece with fewer midtones in between. Be aware of the areas where light directly hits an element in a drawing. Element refers to any object in the drawing. For example, the bird, twigs, leaves, and the berries are all elements of the drawing below.

High value contrast can create a dynamic and visually striking effect, making certain elements stand out prominently. This contrast can be used to draw attention to specific areas, create focal points, or emphasize particular elements in a composition.

Low Contrast value refers to more diffuse lighting where there are little or no hot spots or heavy dark shadows in the art piece. You will be using the full range of values in a low contrast drawing.

Low value contrast involves minimal differences in lightness or darkness between elements, resulting in a more subtle and harmonious visual experience. This approach is often used for creating softer and more cohesive designs or to convey a camouflage of sorts.

In the context of design, art, or aesthetics, the term "value" refers to the degree of the light and shadow that are illuminating the form. Value contrast occurs when there is a noticeable difference in the lightness or darkness between two adjacent elements or forms in a drawing.

Artists use a value scale to train their artistic eye to differentiate the values of lightness or darkness of a shape. The value scale is a simple tool to help train you to see the correct light or dark areas in an image or photo that you are trying to duplicate with a pencil.

Using the value scale

Place your Value Scale over an area on the image that you wish to duplicate. The goal is to match the level of lightness or darkness with what you see in the hole or window of the value scale. Move the window over to the area on your drawing to see if you have reached the same value. Voila! Contrast Perfection!

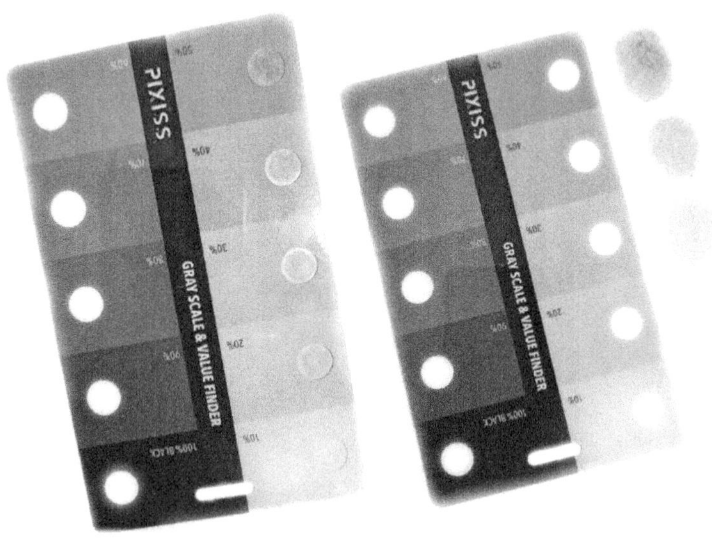

You can use this scale specifically when drawing from another image or from life. I would even suggest that you will use your Value Scale throughout your artistic endeavors. Your value scale is one of the most important tools in your artist toolkit.

Many artists have trouble judging exactly how dark a shadow may be. The reason the Value Scale is so important is that it gives you a baseline from which you can judge everything and train your eye to see the subtle differences in form shadows. You need it! I still use my Value Scale. Sometimes an old school tool is the most perfect tool.

The best technique for creating value variation is with your smudge stick. The easiest method for using your smudge stick is to draw lines on scrap paper and rub your smudge stick over your scribbles. Notice that it will pick up the marks of graphite from the scrap paper.

Use the smudge stick to shade or draw soft edge lines when creating form elements on your sketchbook paper. Your smudge stick is far easier to erase than pencil marks so if you are in doubt about what you want to do, start with your smudge stick.

Exercise 3: Drawing 3D Objects On 2D Paper

A. Draw and shade a Ball, Cone, Block and Tube like those shown below. Choose whether your light source is on the left or the right and shade all with that source only. Your drawing will not match all the images below because they are drawn from two different light sources. Use your smudge stick for shading.

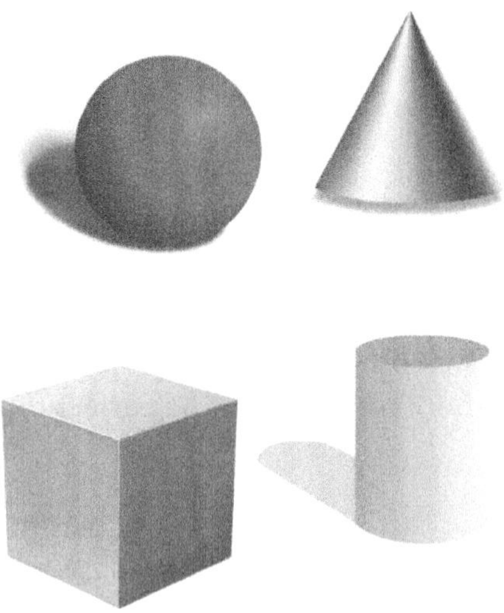

B. Practice turning your 2-D images and cartoons from Exercise 2 into 3-D renderings. Use your smudge stick to blend the forms.

Tip: One trick to get softer or smoother shading with your smudge stick is to shade a patch on scrap paper and transfer the graphite of the pencil with the smudge stick to your drawing.

Transfer the graphite from your scrap paper to the image forms with the smudge stick.

Remember - Keep your grubby fingers off the paper!
Practice creating smooth transitions between light and shadow using your smudge sticks to shade all of your cartoons.

C. Draw a new 2-D cartoon. Shade it to make a **high contrast** image of the cartoon you just drew. Use your pencil for drawing the shapes and shading the darkest part by holding your pencil sideways to shade a wider swath. Smooth the whole thing with your smudge stick only. There should be very dark areas and very light areas in your cartoon image.

D. Draw the same cartoon image again using only your smudge stick to draw it.. In this exercise, you will only use your pencil on your scrap paper. Lay down a thick layer of graphite on the scrap. Then use the small pointy smudge stick to draw the same shape forms from the previous exercise. Switch to a bigger smudge stick and create the shading in order to produce a **low contrast** image.

An example of Higher and Lower Contrast shading.

Conclusion

Understanding how light and shadow can create many levels of value is a journey that takes practice and observation. As you progress, you'll develop a keen eye for how light interacts with the world around you. We will also cover that in Chapter 5 so, grab your sketchbook and experiment with value and let your drawings come to life!

Chapter 4: Texture

Artistic expression knows no bounds, and exploring different styles is an exciting journey that allows you to discover your unique voice as an artist. In this chapter, we will delve into the world of artistic styles, encouraging you to experiment with diverse approaches, techniques, and influences to find the style that resonates most with your creative vision.

Texture plays a pivotal role in bringing your drawings to life, adding depth, richness, and a tactile quality to your artwork. You can elevate your drawings by incorporating texture and capturing intricate details in various values.

Texture refers to the surface quality of an object, whether it's smooth, rough, bumpy, or soft. In drawings, creating a sense of texture can evoke emotions, provide context, and enhance suggested realism. Different textures can be achieved through various drawing techniques.

There are four primary methods of creating texture in a drawing. In this chapter we will examine those methods which are called, **Hatching**, **Cross-Hatching**, **Stippling**, and **Blending.**

The primary tool of creating texture is **Line Variation. Hatching and Cross-Hatching** involves drawing parallel lines to create shading, while cross-hatching adds intersecting lines to enhance depth and texture. Varying the spacing, angle, and density of your hatch marks can mimic different textures, from the smoothness of skin to the roughness of tree bark.

Stippling is the technique of creating texture by using small dots, which in effect are very short lines. The density and arrangement of dots can convey different surfaces, from the fine texture of sand to the coarse texture of a rock. Stippling requires patience but can result in intricate and visually interesting effects.

Blending is most realistic and involves smoothly transitioning between different tones or textures. It's achieved using **blending stumps or smudge sticks**. Blending is particularly useful for creating realistic textures in objects like fabrics, fur, or skin.

The following image is a value scale that also shows examples of each of the techniques described above. Many artists choose one or more of these methods to create texture in their work. I use smudge sticks for skin but often will use hashing or stippling as well for fabrics or any other texture I wish to depict. There are no rules for texture so try everything!

HATCHING

white | mid-value | black

CROSS-HATCHING

white | mid-value | black

STIPPLING (POINTILLISM)

white | mid-value | black

BLENDING

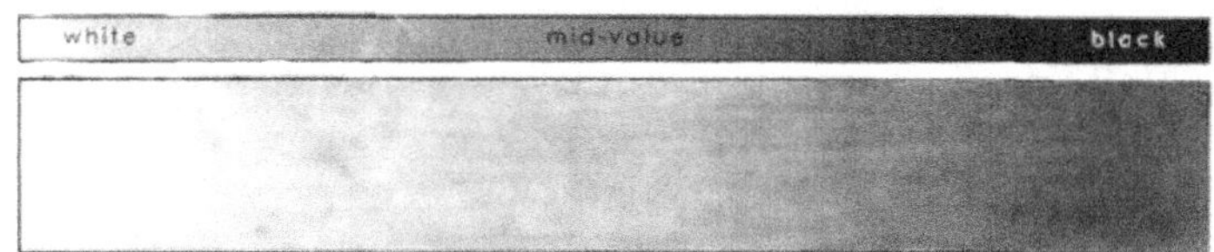

Shadows and highlights add depth and dimension to your drawings. Whether blending, stippling, hatching or cross-hatching, try building up layers of details gradually. Start with broad strokes to establish the overall structure, then add finer details as you progress.

Exercise 4

A. Draw four circles. Choose which side the light is on – left or right. Use hatch and crosshatch lines to shade the first two circles. If the light is on the left, the darker shadows will be on the right.

B. Then with the light source on the opposite side, shade the other circles using stippling for the third and shade the fourth circle using your smudge stick.

Conclusion

Texture, value shading, and details are the tools that transform a flat, two-dimensional drawing into a sensory experience. Whether you're aiming for hyper-realism or exploring stylized representations, the thoughtful use of texture will add a new dimension to your artistic expression. Embrace the tactile nature of your drawings and let your creativity flourish.

Chapter 5: The Nature of Light

So how do you know where to put the lightest light, the darkest darks and all those tones in between? Well, it all depends on the type of lighting.

Let's start by analyzing the basics of light. Light can be categorized into two different types. **Natural Light** is sunlight, and **Artificial Light** is from lamps or other sources. As artists, we are particularly interested in how any light illuminates and wraps objects creating various tones and highlights.

Light sources create highlights, shadows and all-important mid-tones, all of which add the third dimension to your drawings. Learning to observe and replicate the way light interacts with **Form elements** is essential for any artist. Remember, form elements are those objects you draw, like a car or a bird or a book. Notice whether the light reflecting is sharp and crisp or if it's diffuse. Often crisp lighting means higher contrast drawing and harder edges on lines.

Shadows

Shadows can be broadly categorized into two types: Form Shadows and Cast Shadows. Both types are essential to understanding Three-Dimensional drawing and the nature of light.

Form Shadows

Form shadows occur on the surface of an object that is turned away from the light source. They are the more subtle shadows that exist on the object itself, as opposed to cast shadows. Form shadows are often not as dark but are the magical ingredient for creating a 3-D form of whatever you are drawing. Understanding form shadows is crucial for rendering realistic and believable drawings. In this first image, both the faces and her arm are not complete. It makes them look more like incomplete sketches.

Notice the difference when the subtle form shadows are added to complete the 3-D illusion of depth and roundness. Now it resembles a completed rendering in 3-D. Did you notice the hot spot on the man's head? The light source is top right and a little forward.

Form shadows define the individual characteristics of anything and every object you see.

Tip: Lightly sketch a small sun on the paper roughly in the area of your desired light source. This is usually in the upper left or upper right corner. It helps to remember the direction of light so that you never have shadows cast at the wrong angle. When done drawing, erase the small sun.

Take note of the H**ot Spots** (also called sunspots) on the objects that you are drawing. **Hot spots** are where the light is most intense and looks almost like a sparkle on the object like when you see sparkles on the water on a sunny day. Highlights add sparkle to your artwork and are like the cherry on top of a sundae.
In this image you can see the Hot spots primarily in the eyes of the cedar waxwing birds. However, you can also see that the wingtips, foreheads and shoulders are highlighted too.

Identifying the light source in your drawing is crucial. The direction, intensity, and angle of the light source greatly impacts the way the light will wrap around an object or how shadows are cast. Take note of whether the light is coming from above, below, or from the side. This awareness will influence the placement and shape of both the object and its shadows.

In diffuse lighting, whether you have a softening filter on a lamp or outside on a cloudy day, you will have lots more subtle mid-tones and shades in your drawing. There will be fewer hard lines and edges and few, if any hot spots. This is when most edge lines are drawn with your smudge stick – not your pencil. Diffuse lighting is referred to as low contrast.

In this portrait of "Sisters," I used my smudge stick to soften almost all the edges to give the feeling of sweetness to the art piece.

Cast Shadows

Cast shadows are the dark shapes created when an object blocks the path of light and always exist on surfaces opposite the light source. They can provide depth and dimension to your drawings as well as anchor your artwork in reality. Pay attention to the shape and length of cast shadows, as they change based on the object's form and the angle of the light.

Notice the shadows cast on the ground by the building and on the building under the eaves of the roof. There are also cast shadows on the floor of the porch as well as the steps. Cast shadows connect objects to their environment and anchor the art in reality.

Where do you think the light source is? Can you tell from the angle of the shadows? Can you tell which way the wind is blowing? All of these questions can be answered by looking carefully at the image. The more questions that can be asked and answered in any art piece, the more interesting it is to the viewer.

Hint: The wind is blowing from the opposite direction as the light.

Mapping Light

Light travels in straight lines but will also appear to wrap an object. Yep, I hear those eyeballs rolling around your head again. If light travels in a straight line, then how can it possibly wrap around an object? You don't have to learn physics or be a math guru to figure this out. It's simple, really. It's a trick of the light, which like all art is magic! Well, sort of.

It's caused by reflection! Reflected light, also called bounced light, illuminates the shadow side of an object. This phenomenon is what you learn to use in order to enhance the realism of your drawings.

Here's the basic anatomy of light and form.

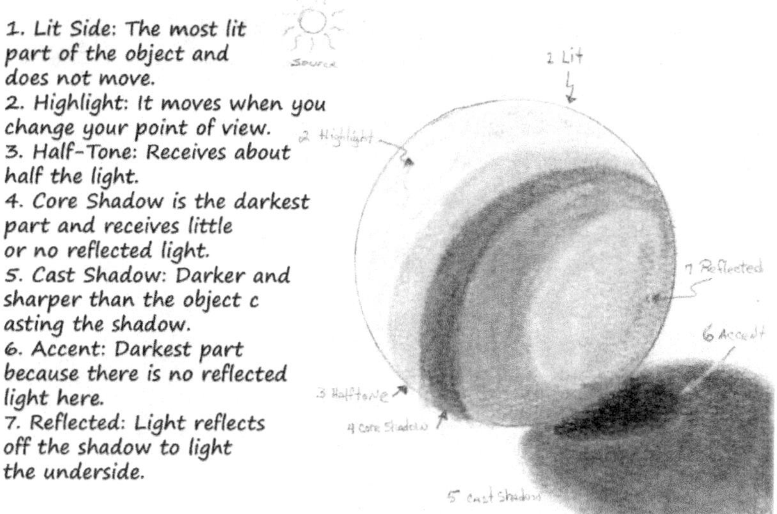

This is both informational and helpful when drawing a high detail image where the value of the light and shadow is important to make your rendering realistic. You can turn a 2D object into 3-D by understanding how light wraps an object and shading is the method to do it. Now, with a little shading and light we have objects that appear to be three-dimensional. Practice blending and creating shadows on your sketches. You'll be amazed at what you can create!

Viewfinder

When looking at something you want to draw, it can seem overwhelming because the image as a whole may seem too complicated. There is a little trick that artists use to keep from feeling like they are seeing too much stuff all at the same time. It's called a viewfinder.

A viewfinder allows you to focus only on a smaller section of the image you want to draw without getting overwhelmed by a lot of shapes, forms, or other elements around what you are trying to draw. It also allows you to see and focus on values of these smaller shapes so that you can create accurate representations on your paper.

I sometimes use a viewfinder to draw only one fourth of the whole picture at a time. It helps to keep from feeling overwhelmed by too much stuff to see and draw at once.

Tip: Create a viewfinder. I like to use a scrap of paper with a square or rectangle hole cut into it. This allows me to isolate what I want to draw and disregard all the extra info in the scene.

Exercise 5 – Contrast & Shadow

In these exercises, you will be applying many of the skills you have learned so far. Take your time.

A. Choose any high contrast image with hard cast shadows. Keep it simple, you are not trying to draw a whole scene, just one object with a shadow. You could find an image on the internet or work from a black and white photo. If possible, print the image and use it as a reference photo. Make sure the image is high contrast. Sketch it in your drawing journal. If it seems overwhelming, create a viewfinder and sketch smaller parts of the object at a time. Look for those balls, cubes, cones and tubes in the image form you are sketching. Use your smudge sticks, pencils and value scale to try and duplicate the shadows and hotspots. Spend some time building up layers to achieve the proper value. Add cast shadow. Match the values of your drawing to the values of the object and shadows using your value scale.

B. Choose any low contrast object and sketch it in your journal. If possible, print the image and match the values using your value scale. Try to focus on softer edges and all the mid tones using only your smudge stick. Use your pencils only on the scrap paper. Perhaps you will want to experiment with texture. Match the values of your drawing to the values of the image using your value scale and shade it accordingly.

Conclusion

Adding detail is about capturing the subtleties and nuances of your subject, making it more engaging. Observe the play of light and shadow, the tiny variations in value, and the intricacies of surface textures. You have all the tools you need to draw amazing works of art. The key at this point in the process is to be patient and practice using your tools and skills as much as possible. Daily practice is preferred but not required. The more you practice using your tools, the faster you will see results. Your creativity and skillset will soar!

Chapter 6: Composition

Up to this point, we've been focused on drawing an object, which is a collection of shapes that create a form of something such as a person, or a thing. That sounds sort of like a noun, right? Are we building sentences or pictures?

Let's examine that. A form of something or even a collection of forms would be persons, places or things, all of which are known as nouns or the characters of the story. We're going to step up our game a bit to drawing multiple forms and arranging them into a cohesive art piece that helps create a story. As with any story, it's constructed with sentences.

We've all heard that a picture is worth a thousand words. When we create a picture, a drawing, painting or whatever, we are *composing* a story – a flash fiction or flash non-fiction of our artistic perception of a moment in time.

In a writer's world, the term "flash fiction" is a story of about a thousand words. It's also called a composition.

In the world of art, making choices in how you arrange shapes and forms (nouns or characters) on your paper or canvas along with how you present those forms (adjectives) and how they all interact (verbs) are crucial for conveying meaning (sentences and stories). Guiding the viewer's eye (the plot), and creating a harmonious visual experience (making them want to read the story) is called Composition. Art is "composed" in a similar manner as a writer, composing a story.

Why is this important? Well, the truth is…artists are just like writers, we like to tell stories. Don't roll those eyes at me. It's true! Great art can tell a detailed story in the mind of the viewer just as compelling as if the artist had written a thousand-word story.

The first choice you make is whether you want to do a piece in a portrait or a landscape format. This is also known as vertical or horizontal formatting. Vertical or Portrait format is *often* used (but not always) to showcase an individual object form like a person or animal or some other noun. The Horizontal or Landscape format would most often be used for rendering a scene composed with multiple object forms (nouns) that may have more than one focal point.

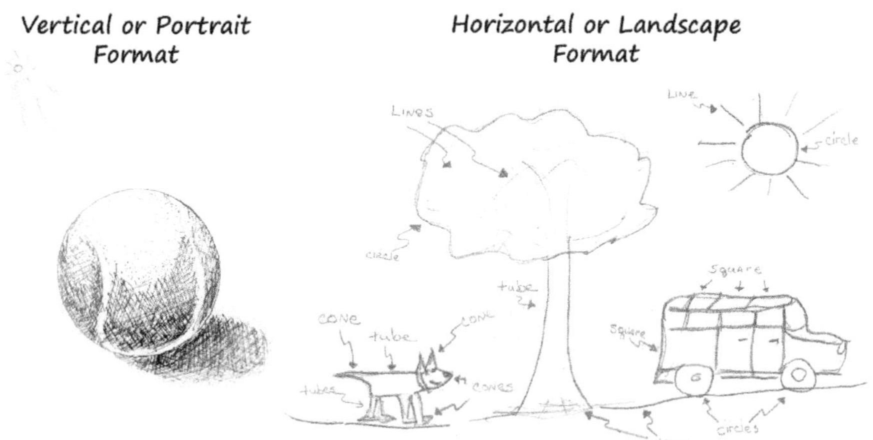

On the right is Hubby's drawing of our grandson on his way to school.

I asked my husband for a picture of our grandson going to school in the mornings. While my husband is an engineer, he was able to create a little story showing how the dog escorts the boy to the bus stop in the early hours, where he waits under the tree for the bus. The bus takes him to school and the dog now has to wait for him to return. It's a good enough story that I want to use in my book and he's not even an artist or a writer. He's an electronic engineer and even he can be artistic!

In this chapter, we will explore the principles of composition and layout, providing you with the tools to enhance your artistic expression and control the way your audience views your work, which allows you to tell a compelling story with your art.

Separating Space In Your Composition.

The easiest way to figure out the best composition is to separate your space. Let's start separating by using a common artistic method of outlining the story you are trying to tell in your art piece.

Rule of Thirds

One of the most widely recognized principles of composition is the **Rule of Thirds**. Imagine dividing your canvas into a grid of nine equal sections by drawing two horizontal and two vertical lines. The points where the lines intersect create **Focal Points**, which are four potential places that you can choose to guide the view of your audience.

**** All the subsequent images in this chapter show the *Rule of Thirds* grid overlay.**

A **Focal Point** is where you want to place the most important part of your drawing. If what you're drawing has eyes, they will always be a focal point and should be located on the page near one of those four intersections and inside the center square. It's what would be the primary character of your story.

A **Focal Point** that is slightly off center creates visual interest. This is not a rule. It's more of a strong suggestion. This subconsciously prompts the viewer to look there first then all around the art for other interesting things.

Artists are control freaks. It's true! An artist can control how you view their work in the same way a writer reveals a story. It all starts with making the main character the focal point of the art piece. That is how the magic happens. This is the first of many little tricks showing how an artist can control just how you view their work of art and what emotions they can evoke.

Tip: Avoid placing your focal point at the exact center. The exact center is boring for the viewer. In writing, it would represent a lack of character development. Slightly off center creates visual interest for the artist's story.

If your drawing is still life or abstract, you should decide what is the most important part of what you're drawing and place it near one of those Rule of Thirds intersections. It should also be the sharpest and most detailed part of your drawing. Make sure it is in focus. This is not a rule. It's a method of controlling the story that you want to tell with your art. Learning how to use these suggestions is a great benefit to making art that people are sure to love and gaining the skills to know when to deviate from suggested practices will make your work inspiring.

Regions

I like to define my space into regions. Those regions are Background, Midground, Foreground, Focal Points, and Negative Space. You may not use all of these regions in every drawing, but typically you will always have one or more focal points and some of the other four regions in your drawing. Continuing with the "telling a story" analogy, the regions may contain supporting characters (forms) for your story and act as *modifiers or adjectives* in the story that you are telling. You need those details to make the story clear.

Things that are the farthest away in your composition are called **Background.** That is often where you have mountains, clouds and the horizon in landscapes. One thing to note is that things in the background are often rendered out of focus or not quite as sharp. Some would say that you are "setting the scene."

Midground is where things begin to come into focus and is often (but not always) where you will place the focal point(s) of your drawing. You can have multiple focal points. I recommend that if you have more than one, they should be diagonally across from each other and not side by side. Diagonals make more visually interesting compositions. Diagonals imply conflict between the most important characters or climax of the story the artist is telling.

Foreground is whatever is in front of the Midground, and it can be a focal point or be things like framing elements that lead the viewer deeper into the picture or art story. **Framing elements** within your composition draw attention to the main subject. This could be natural elements like branches and leaves. Some artists use flora or architectural elements like doorways or arches. The framing in the foreground will also add another layer of depth to your artwork.

Things in the foreground can be in focus or not. Think of a camera view. It all depends on the depth of field. As the artist, you get to decide how deep your field of view will be.

Negative Space is the area or space around forms (nouns) or between elements within the composition. It can be white space, repeated patterns or out of focus background elements. While it's called "negative" space, it is a positive and essential aspect of visual design. Negative space helps define what is important and gives the viewer's eye a place to rest. Have you ever heard someone say that a picture is "too busy?" The term "too busy" suggests that there is not enough negative space to balance the composition.

Artists and designers often use negative space intentionally to guide the viewer's focus and emphasize the subject. How do they do that? The trick is that negative space is often a little blurry or out of focus as compared to "the object form" the artist wants you to focus upon. Pay attention to how negative space can enhance your composition, creating a sense of balance and allowing your viewer's eye to rest.

Blank or negative space creates balance. Sometimes the Framing element and the Focal Point are in the Foreground space which are rendered more sharp and clear. Midground elements are out of focus and Negative space is in the Background.

In this image, the entire **Background** is **Negative Space**. The **Midground** flora is out of focus and the **Focal Point** as well as some small part of the **Framing** flora is in the **Foreground.**

There's a lot going on in the image below. The bird sitting on the diagonal branch in the foreground is expanding the depth of field and focus and *leading* the viewer deeper into the composition. Notice how the background is blurry. The midground is sharp and clear with all of the birds in focus. The birds are looking at each other in the midground, directing the viewer to the three primary focal points in the central square.

See how the viewer is guided around the entire composition to notice all the birds and focal points in both the midground and the foreground. That guidance is done with *Leading Lines.*

Leading Lines are a compositional technique that involves using lines within your drawing to guide the viewer's eye toward a specific focal point or area of interest. They create a sense of direction or flow within your drawing. They act as visual pathways that guide your viewer's gaze through your artwork.

Consider the placement and orientation of these lines to direct attention where you want it. Leading Lines are the *verbs* in the story that you are telling in your art.

In this image we see that the soaring raven is in focus. The bird exists in the midground. In this image, there is nothing indicating foreground. The clouds in the background are blurry and quite non-descript. However, they are important for visual interest. The entire **Background** is **Negative Space**.

If you look carefully, you can see the clouds are laid out in an "S" curve pattern. Ok, in this case it's more of a "Z" shape but the effect is the same. It creates *Leading Lines* that help guide the viewer's eye through the whole image. The wings as well as the bird's body drawn on *Diagonals* cause the eye to zip back up to the top of the "Z" and look again.

Diagonals are very powerful in a drawing and can be the strongest verb in the artistic arsenal for telling your story. They are visually interesting and can create leading lines that guide the viewer's eye around your composition.

Sometimes, leading lines converge or meet at a specific point in the composition. This convergence point creates a powerful focal point in your drawing and may indicate the protagonist in your visual story. Placing important elements, such as the main subject or a significant detail, at this point can draw attention and create a strong clear impact.

Notice how the lines of the tree enter the scene and guide your eye around the image. The eyes of the subject are leading lines too. Whatever they look at will lead the viewer to look there too.

The tree limb creates a visually interesting diagonal that leads to the tail of the mother, guiding the eye down to her face which is a focal point looking at her babies. This creates an implied line to the other focal point in the scene, those babies. It all implies a story of mother and child relationship in the animal world, suggesting a thematic element to your artistic story.

Now, you have another trick in your arsenal for creating an artistic story. You can use any of these tricks to create themes or to direct the viewer to look at certain things longer in your drawing. It's amazing how powerful and knowledgeable you have become in telling artistic stories already. It all starts with lines on paper.

Experiment with different types of lines—straight, curved, diagonal, or zigzag. Each type of line can convey a different mood or energy. Diagonal lines, for example, can suggest movement or dynamism, while horizontal lines may evoke a sense of calm or stability. While actual lines are explicit and defined, implied lines are suggested by the arrangement of shapes, objects, or even the gaze of a character within the drawing. These lines can be equally as effective in leading the viewer's eye.

Thumbnails

Sometimes, when you are not sure how to build a composition, you can use thumbnails, which are small quick sketches. This should not be a long process, since they are small. Spend a few minutes for each thumbnail, to see what works, and what does not. Sketching multiple **thumbnail drawings** can help you explore various arrangements or characters before committing to a final piece that tells the story you want to tell.

Thumbnails are also the best use for all that scrap paper you've got laying around. I often buy quality paper that is more than twice the size that I need because it's cheaper to buy that way. I invested in a paper cutter and cut it myself. I always end up with small scraps that I can use for thumbnails or practice pieces, thus utilizing all of my investment.

The little thumbnails below are called "inchies." They are simply scraps of paper that are one or two inch squares that I keep around to sketch ideas for scenes or stories that I may want to write or illustrate. Don't be afraid to experiment with different compositions.

Exercise 6

A. Start with creating some Thumbnail sketches. Sketch a tree on a hill or in a field or park using the Rule of Thirds.

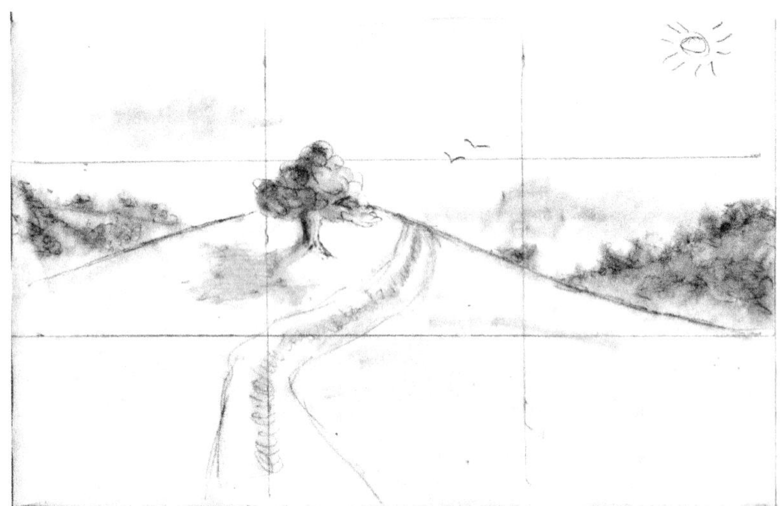

B. Sketch a tree on the hill or in a field with mountains in the background.
C. Sketch the tree on the hill or on a sand dune with the ocean in the background.
D. Sketch the tree with leaves and branches in the foreground and whatever you prefer in the background

Conclusion

Mastering composition opens up a world of possibilities for artistic expression and storytelling. Play with thumbnails. Get in the habit of creating thumbnails before every drawing. Embrace the freedom to explore and discover your unique voice in the language of art.

Chapter 7: Proportion

Where Composition allows you to introduce characters in your story, proportion guides the creation or framework of each character and how they fit together in the scene. Proportion identifies the size of each object form, the distance from one another, and how each relates to other forms in the scene.

It's not just realism that benefits. Illustrators for comics, television, web developers, gamers, architects and more all have to develop skills in proportion. In this chapter, we will delve into some simple techniques for measuring and comparing proportions.

Form Proportion

How do we understand the importance of proportion? Well…we can start with defining proportion. For our purposes, proportion is the size of something as compared to what is normal or compared to another. For us that means that the size of one part of a form will have a normal size for other parts of the same form. Confused? Let's look at an example.

The human body is typically about eight heads tall and three heads wide. Note that this is a generalization. People are different and some are only seven and a half heads tall. However, for an artist, eight heads in a body is a good standard. That would sure make a strange sound bite in a marketing campaign, eh? I digress…Let's get back on point.

Here you can see that the human body is approximately eight heads tall and three heads wide. The torso is also about three heads high. Note the size of the arms and legs. Armpit to elbow is one head length, as is elbow to wrist. Hip to knee is two heads in length, as is knee to ankle.

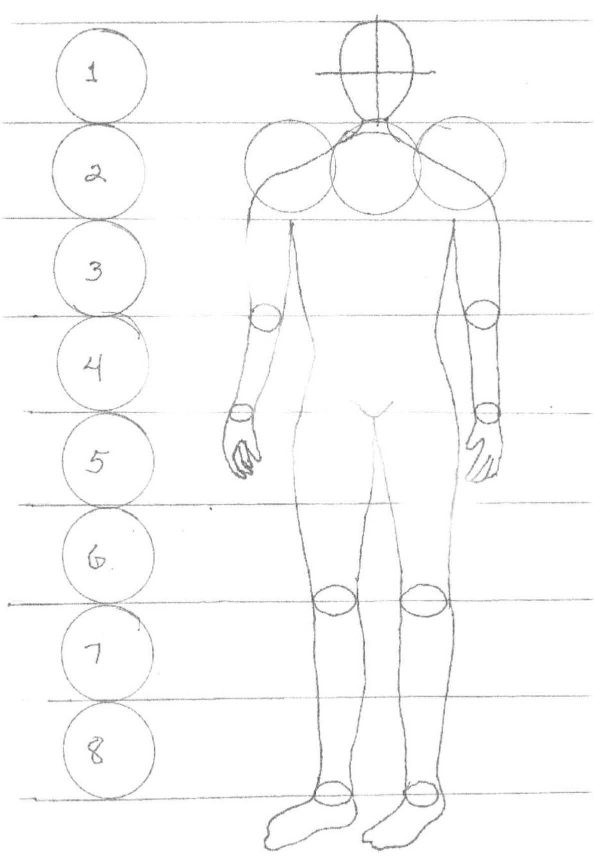

You can find the proportions of just about any form that you want to draw on-line by searching: "*X* proportions for drawing" or "X proportions for artists." "*X*" is whatever you want to draw – a bear or any mammal, a bird, a fish, etc. It is helpful living in the internet age. I didn't grow up with that but certainly appreciate it! We had to buy books on anatomy back in the old days.

There are times when we examine a painting or work of art that is considered a "masterpiece" and can't help but think; "Huh…why?" Ok, some have used other words but, whatever. It still means the same thing. "That's weird" or "That's blatantly wrong" or "that's out of proportion." There are other times when we know something is off even if we can't always figure out what's wrong. But it's still a masterpiece and we are sometimes at a loss to understand why. Well, art is not always perfect. A masterpiece may not be perfect, but it is awesome and masterful in all the ways that matter for the time.

For example, let's look at Botticelli's **The Birth Of Venus**

In Botticelli's masterpiece, notice how delicate and smooth Venus' skin and features are, as well as how her hair mirrors her ample curves as it drapes around her body. There's a lot of other symbolism but let's just try and focus on the proportions of her form for this point. All the goddesses have proportion issues. Can you spot them?

In this image, their arms are quite long. Also, I don't know about you, but I can't drop my shoulder down below my breast like the goddess on the left. She is a goddess, though. Anyway, Venus and the goddess on the right both have forearms that are almost a half head too long.

Even with these issues, it's still a master work of art. These goddesses are stylized and idealized; portrayed as "perfect" for the time in which the master painted them.

Tip: This is also a life lesson. Anything you do should never be an exercise in attempting perfection. Perfection is a perception of the time period, and those perceptions change. As a result, perfection can never be achieved by mere humans. You should instead focus on identifying what is important in the story of your art first, then do it. That is what makes a masterpiece.

Being aware of the form proportions in your drawing is important. You can make informed decisions about stylized drawings via modified proportions once you can master getting the body proportions right in any configuration. By that I mean that you should be able to draw it properly in any position, such as sitting, dancing, or acrobatics before you fiddle with funky or otherwise stylized proportions. You should know how to apply the standards before you presume to disregard them.

Scene Proportions

Next you need to compare the proportions of the object forms within your artwork. More distant objects are smaller than objects in the foreground and sometimes overlap to help indicate their distance.

Use handy tools to measure distances between things of different or similar sizes at different distances. If things are moving in and out of your scene, snap a photo on your phone so that you have a reference when the scene changes.

In the scene below, the head of the cowboy in the foreground is bigger than the entire body of the cowboy behind him. The cowboy in the midground is more than twice the size of the man on a horse in the background.

Use your pencil or a ruler held out at arm's length to judge roughly the different size of things in the scene. It's important to always hold your measuring device at arm's length so that you get an accurate and similar reading each time you check.

By measuring the head of the cowboy in the foreground, you can judge the size of someone else some distance away in the midground or background of a scene. Over time and with practice, you the artist learn to see proportions in the distance of scenes. This is why drawing scenes from life is so important. You learn that one human on a horse can look half the size of a human in the midground.

Exercise 7 Proportions

A. **Define the form proportions of a cat using your phone or computer.** Start by searching on-line for a cat silhouette. Choose one you like and figure out the cat proportions. The image you choose must show the full head and body.

B. In the following image, there is a small scrap of paper that I use as a rough baseline measurement of the cat's head. Figure out the cat proportions for the cat that you found on-line using a scrap of paper to create a baseline measurement of the cat head.

C. How many cat heads make a whole cat? This is an approximation, just like the eight heads to make a human.

D. Draw your cat as if it were the focal point of a scene. Remember to use the rule of thirds. The primary form in your sketch is the cat you chose to draw in Exercise A. Now use your completed sketch of the cat form to define the proportions of other forms. Draw your cat with something else in the scene.

Pretend you are telling a story about the cat that you chose, and you are trying to illustrate it. Maybe draw a tree in the distant background or a bush with a bird in the mid-ground or you could draw a cat toy. Use your imagination.

Conclusion

Whether you are working in a realistic manner or with a more stylized rendition, you need to understand proportion and how to figure out the form proportions of the creature and the scene you are trying to represent. Once you have a grasp of how proportions play a significant role in the development of your artistic skillset, you will find creative ways to "play" or "twist" conventional proportions to help with the story of your artwork.

Chapter 8: Linear Perspective

Linear Perspective is a magical ingredient that can add both depth and realism to your drawings. There are a lot of different ways to introduce this subject. My plan is to explore some of the principles of perspective drawing; that is, how objects appear in space and the techniques to create convincing spatial relationships in your artwork.

This is by no means the definitive answer to mathematical perspective. I am teaching from an artistic design point of view. I'm not saying I have the math mind of a tomato, but math was not my major in college. My degree is in the Arts.

While there are other views in this theory, I've been doing this a long time and am offering my more simplistic view of this model. My approach will allow you to gain a deeper understanding of perspective and how it contributes to the realism of your drawings without the panic inspired by mathematical equations.

So, here's the deal. **Linear perspective or One Point Perspective** is where parallel lines converge toward a single **vanishing point**. This creates the illusion of depth in your drawings. Remember way back at the beginning, when we drew those parallel lines that were closer at the top? We turned them into roads, railroad tracks or rivers. That is linear perspective in a nutshell. Let's examine that a bit more.

In each linear perspective drawing, there is at least one **vanishing point** (VP). A **vanishing point** is a dot on the **Horizon Line** where all parallel lines meet, called **Convergence Lines**. To the human eye, although they are parallel, they seem to meet at a great distance.

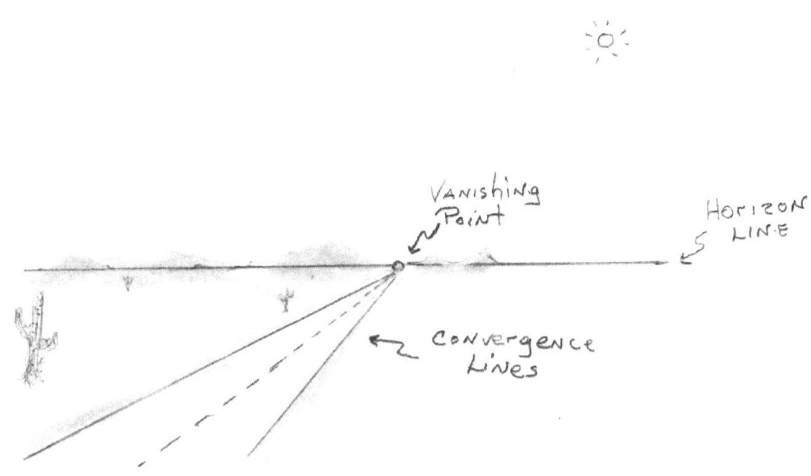

First, we need to understand the concept of a **horizon line** and a **vanishing point**. These concepts are foundational to any **point perspective**. Simple forms in one-point perspective would be mastering cubes, tubes, and cones, which lays the groundwork for more complex scenes.

When drawing or painting, the horizon-line's placement has a significant effect on the outcome. You can use your "artistic license" to build different compositions with different horizon line placements.

In general: When the horizon line is near the **center** of a drawing, it translates as **Human Eye view** when looking forward. If the point of view is looking at an angle down, the horizon line will be lower on the page, and it's called a **Bird Eye view**. When it looks as if the viewer is looking up from below, the horizon line will be higher on the page. This is called a **Worm Eye view**.

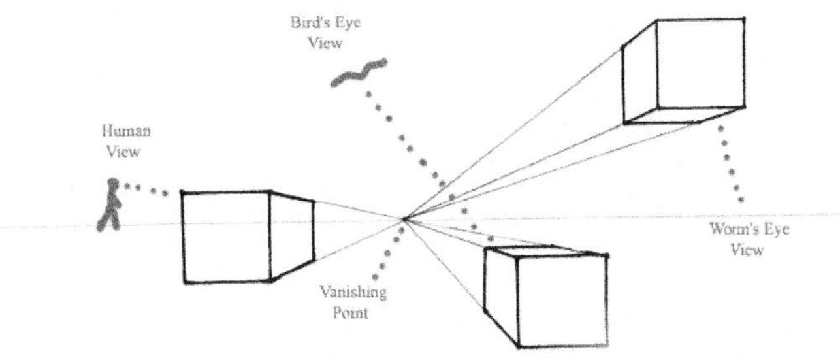

One-point perspective is used for drawing objects that are in front of the observer. The object elements in a scene that have **width lines**, like the cubes in the previous image, will be **parallel to the horizon** and to each other. All those lines vanish at the same point. The **height lines** of those same cubes are **perpendicular to the horizon** and also parallel to each other.

The image below shows a low horizon line, indicating a Bird Eye view with a single Vanishing Point. Next to it is the same image flipped showing the horizon high on the page indicating a Worm Eye view.

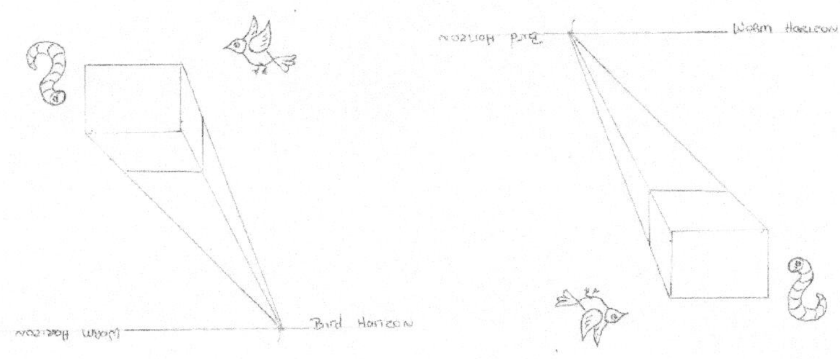

One more thing to consider is **Atmospheric perspective,** which is often used in landscapes. Distant elements appear lighter and less detailed, contributing to the illusion of depth. Overlapping and size variation in the context of atmospheric perspective will add complexity to your drawings. The boys in the following drawing demonstrate an example of an Atmospheric Perspective.

Notice how the boys are in crisp focus and sharp detail. As you look into the background, the scenery gets lighter with less detail, even more so for the farthest trees in comparison to the scrub pines at the edge of the field. You can see actual blades of grass at the boy's feet, but all other grass is out of focus.

One point perspective, point of view and atmospheric perspective is what you should focus on learning at this time. The following is informational.

There are other options/methodology for learning perspective. What I present is a simple user/artist friendly version that is both demonstrative and applicable for most real-world scenarios. I believe that using this simple method will serve your needs and boost your skills to help reach your ultimate goal.

For your information or if curious about point perspectives, here is a visual representation of Two-Point perspective. This perspective is often used in architectural drawing.

In Two-Point perspective, there are two vanishing points along the horizon line.

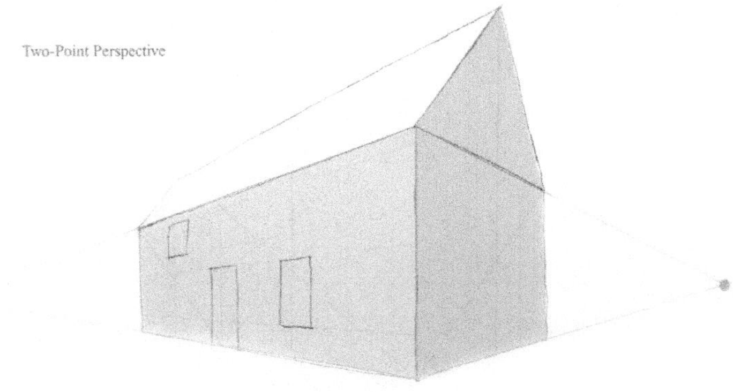

The principle of **two-point perspective** is where two vanishing points guide the convergence lines from two directions to keep everything in proportion.

Three-point perspective is where an additional vanishing point represents height or depth and is used to create bird eye and worm eye views. These viewpoints offer unique perspectives for your drawings.

The third Vanishing Point is called the **Vertical Vanishing Point (VVP)**. It's used when the object is viewed either from **Bird eye** or **Worm eye** point of view. For example, in a Worm eye view, when you look up at a skyscraper, it seems to get smaller the higher you look.

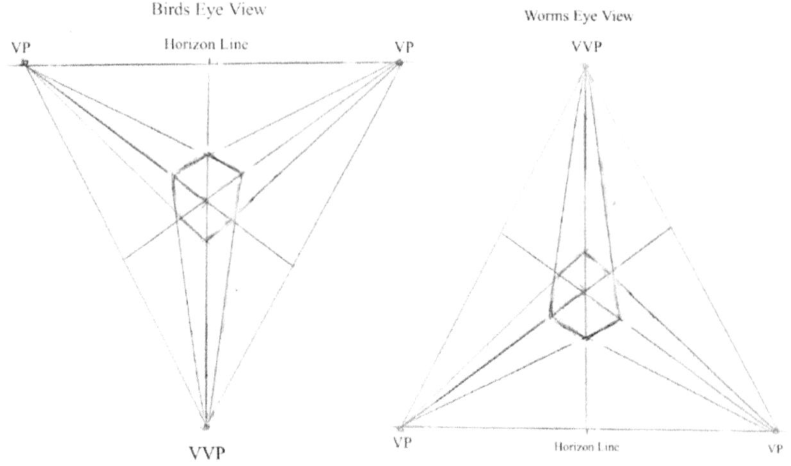

Again, this is informational only. You are not expected to take on this challenge at this time. Still, it doesn't hurt to try seeing the perspective of a bird looking down at a building in the first image from high in the sky. Perhaps in the other image you can imagine a worm looking up at a skyscraper from the point of view of the curb on the street.

Exercise 8

A. Sketch a thumbnail of the tree on a hill from a worm's eye point of view based on this image.

B. Draw a second thumbnail sketch from a bird eye point of view based on this image.

Point-of-view perspectives are a valuable part of the creative process and can lead to unexpected and exciting results. Notice how the first scene is a typical landscape sketch. One might wonder what's down the road or over that hill. The tree and the road are the focal points.

In the Worm-eye view, the thumbnail has a very different feel. There is a mystery here. The focal point is the hole in the tree. Is there something in the hollow tree? The horizon line is near the top third of the image.

In the bird-eye view, you can see a much wider world with more mountains. The tree and the other birds become focal points. The horizon is near the bottom third of the image.

C. Experiment with drawing everyday objects in a scene using linear perspective in your sketchbook. In this exercise, try to stick with a single point perspective and only change your point of view from **human** to **worm** eye view. This exercise will enhance your ability to observe and represent the world around you.

D. Finally render another scene from a **Bird Eye** perspective. Create interest by placing the horizon lower than center.

**In each case, you will need to choose the angle of your light source and a vanishing point along the horizon from each point of view. Try to apply the principles of both linear and atmospheric perspective to your drawings. Remember, in this context and exercise, atmospheric perspective is just making stuff in the background fuzzy or out of focus and lighter using your smudge stick. These are thumbnail exercises and not meant to be great works of art.

For example, I started with a cup of coffee in a coffee shop with a bagel on a table. I drew the cup and bread while sitting and looking at the table to my left. This would be a **Human Eye** point of view, and the horizon is central on the page. There's a big dog staring at bread on the other table. The dog's head is at eye level or a little below that yummy snack.

Here, I can imagine drawing from the dog's point of view, slightly lower than my own and would avoid placing the horizon line in the exact center of the paper. It would be higher on the page. Placement of the forms (cup or bread) are not exactly in the center of the page. Maybe I'd show only the dog's nose in the foreground, or his head resting on the table, trying to smell or snatch that bread. Play with thumbnails of your own sketches and see what point of view you can create.

Conclusion

Whether you're sketching landscapes, or still life, a solid understanding of linear perspective transforms your artwork into a window of three-dimensional imagery onto a two-dimensional space that can tell a story. It's magical!

In time, you may want to try urban sketching or some other type of architectural drawing. If so, you've been introduced already to multiple point perspective concepts that you will need to explore further for that type of artwork. You can always search on-line for more detailed perspective information, if you decide to take on that challenge.

Meanwhile, embrace these creative techniques and enjoy the newfound depth it brings to your creations. You already have so many tools for all kinds of options in your stories of a thousand words!

Chapter 9: Observation & Nature

Drawing from observation is a foundational skill that connects you, the artist, with the world. It involves keen observation of real-life subjects, capturing their essence, and translating them onto paper. Whether it's a serene mountain vista, a lush forest, a peaceful meadow, an alluring beach, or sitting on your balcony sipping tea. Capturing the essence of the moment through art is a fulfilling and immersive experience that encourages appreciation of being in a moment of time that will never exist again. We will explore the techniques to enhance your observational skills, and how this practice can elevate your artistic abilities.

Quick Draw Skills

Let's start with **Contour Drawing.** It involves drawing the outlines of your subject without looking at the paper very much. The idea is to keep your eyes on the image. I use this to hone my quick draw skills. This exercise enhances hand-eye coordination and sharpens observational abilities. This whole chapter is a "working chapter" so there are no exercises at the end. We'll work our way through, so let's get to it.

Find an image on TV that you like and pause the screen. Try to draw a noun (person or thing). Sketch what you see as quickly as you can. Remember to look for those four shapes in whatever you are trying to draw and how lines connect to those shapes. Faces can be circular, blocky, oval, or heart shaped. Use your phone to time yourself for five minutes or set a timer. Trees are most often totally tubular!

Keep trying. You will get better fast. When you get comfortable sketching objects quickly, try drawing them in under three minutes.

Be brave and try it! Learning quick draw skills will be a definite advantage for working outside in changing light conditions and especially for doing those thumbnails.

Try drawing a scene while sitting at a traffic light or sitting in an office. Kind of block in the basic shapes of things first. Then add more lines to define the forms better. Don't worry about too many details or shading. You can add that later if you want. The point is to be fast and loose – not perfect. This is a different skill set you are developing which will help access your creative vision.

The purpose is to capture what is important to convey the scene. Practice this daily. Don't erase anything. Just pretend you don't have an eraser. If you make a mistake and can't incorporate it, just start over. Do this for at least a month until you can comfortably and accurately sketch a scene in three to five minutes. For added challenge, after a few weeks try switching from pencil to black pen. Use hatching or crosshatching for shadows and shading if you want to add those details when working in ink.

Plein Air!

Plein air is a French term that means "go outside and do some art!" Well, that's my interpretation. It actually means "in the open air" and refers to doing art outdoors. So, now it's time to venture outside and try noticing the shapes of something illuminated by natural light. Grab your phone, your sketchpad, book, supplies and let's go outside and do some art.

Tip: The best lighting for any artwork is before 10:00am or after 2:00pm. Longer shadows are better. Shadows create interest and drama.

Plein Air Form drawing allows you to immerse yourself in the environment. Plein air is a valuable practice for honing observational skills and capturing the fleeting beauty of nature.

Spend time (about 15 or 20 minutes) outdoors just observing the object or scene. Pay attention to the play of light and shadow, the colors of the season, and the textures of various elements like grasses and tree bark or leaves in the wind. Even though you are not playing with colors yet, you will notice and learn how colors have different values too and you can translate all that information into your drawing.

Note if it's sunny or cloudy. Is it foggy or drizzly. Maybe it's about to rain. Does the air smell different? Is it warm or is there a brisk chill in the air. Over time, you will be surprised how much more of a story you can create visually by engaging and noticing all of these details of the scene you are about to draw.

Pick an **object** to draw. It could be a tree or a car or a garden statue. Focus on one object and use your phone and take a photo when you first sit down to draw. Are there any "hot spots?" Is the sun warm or is it cold outside? Are there bugs buzzing? Consider adding the bugs into your drawing. Are birds singing or is there lonely silence? Watch and listen. Is your object reflective? If so, what is it reflecting. Can you smell anything. Immerse all of your senses in the moment.

Grab your supplies and a sketchpad and start sketching the object. Take another photo after 15 or 20 minutes.

In the harsh morning light, can you see how the shadows are significantly different in these two photos taken only 15 minutes apart? Continue to watch and study the lighting.

Seeing how light interacts with your subject and how the shape of the cast shadows change is important. Observe any change in the direction of light, shadows, and highlights as the sun moves across the sky.

Slow down and take the time to observe your subject thoroughly. Look carefully and find those cone, block, ball, and tube shapes in the objects and just start sketching. Pay attention to details that might be overlooked in a quick glance. Look for lines and texture that differentiates those details. You may want to add some of that too.
Now, gather up your tools and use them! Wear your glove or use scrap paper to keep your grubby paws off the page. Remember to focus on drawing the shapes you see.

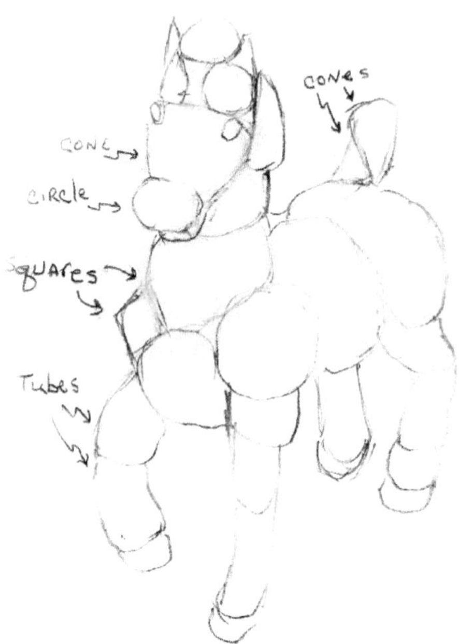

Erase the parts of the lines inside the figure that you will not be using. Keep the parts that show where there are places that define shading changes to use when later adding those details. In my example that would be the horse's muzzle, hair, leg muscles, hooves and the belly.

Use your eraser shield to lighten areas as needed. Try all of your pencils to get the closest shade of gray to the image. Use the brush to remove eraser residue.

Decide if you want to shade using hatch, crosshatch, stippling, smudge stick or any combination of all.
Use the Value Scale to help you achieve the same level of shading for each section of the figure and its shadows.

Do those final details at the end, referring to images on your phone. Pick the image with the best cast shadows and add those details after your form shadows are done. You can refer to your phone image to check your work. Compare your drawing to the image on your phone.

****Remember** – Your drawing is not supposed to look exactly like the photo. Your phone is just a tool, like a pencil or a smudge stick. You have a creative eye that a phone does not have, so whatever you see and create using your human eye will always look far more fascinating to every human out there than any machine.

Match the shading to your value scale for each part of the form. If there are any cast shadows, use your value scale to do those as well. Add texture to enhance your drawing. If there's fur or hair, try hatch strokes or lines. If there's bark, try crosshatch for shading and stippling. Experiment!

You can do this!

Tip: When working outside in natural light, use your phone and take a photo every 15 or 20 minutes as you work.

Plein Air Scene

Now pick a scene and draw a landscape. Your goal is capturing the energy and immediacy of the scene. This is where that quick draw practice comes in handy. Use your phone and take a picture of the scene as you intend to draw it. Edit picture to remove all color to make it easier to see the shapes and values. Now you have a record of the light and the shadows that are cast at that moment.

It's important to note, especially when working plein air, you don't have to draw everything you see. More importantly, you can adjust the placement of something to make a better composition, which is a superb time to employ **thumbnails** or use a **viewfinder**.

Try sketching three thumbnails of the scene. The first should accurately depict what you see. The second shows what it would look like if it was a perfect scene. By that, I mean that if the focal point was in the right spot, or a bird was flying through or that tree was not dead, or the metal fence had wood fence posts instead or the person in the city scene is at the focal point. It could be any of those things. Pick something else to change or fix for the third thumbnail. Maybe sit down and change your point of view. Then choose how you want to see the scene in your final art piece.

You may want to lightly sketch in the rule of thirds grid. Draw the scene as quickly and as best you can. Time yourself for 15 or 20 minutes. Focus on getting the composition arranged and all of the shape/forms in proportion. Remember that you can move things around to make a great composition.

Take another photo of the scene you are trying to draw. Notice how the lighting and shadows have changed. Try getting your perspective right at this stage of drawing. Spend another 15 or 20 minutes trying to add form shadows and clarifying your focal point. Worry about fine details later, like texture, and cast shadows.

Once that's complete, take a final photo of the scene. The light and shadows will have changed again, significantly. Choose the photo you like best and adjust your drawing to represent that photo. Spend another 15 or 20 minutes, adding cast shadows, texture and other final touches to your drawing based on that chosen image. This process is how most plein air competitions are run. Typically, a competition quick draw event is timed for a maximum of 2 hours and those two hours will include other types of artists like painters as well!

I like to do quick draw events in one hour or less. It gives me the opportunity to choose two scenes or points of view to draw and decide later which artwork to submit as an entry to the judges. This is informational, in case you want to strive for a double goal.

Tip: Cast shadows get shorter in the morning and longer in the evening.

Conclusion

Drawing from observation is a skill that evolves over time. Continuously challenge yourself with new subjects and scenarios. Going outside (Plein Air) is the key to understanding the intricacies of form, light, shadow, and texture. Drawing from observation enables you to depict the world with accuracy, bringing a sense of authenticity and depth to your artwork. Whether you're drawing a still life, a portrait, or a landscape, the act of closely observing your subject and the atmosphere informs your artistic decisions and enhances your ability to represent it convincingly and tell a compelling story. You must *be in the moment* with all of your senses to capture that moment for the audience.

The benefits of drawing and observation extend beyond technical skill. It enhances your ability to see the world with a heightened awareness, your unique vision, and by fostering a deeper connection between you and your surroundings.

As the artist, YOU have the power to create a scene the way you want it to be seen. Feel free to move that tree over a few inches or a few feet if you want. You can compose a couple sitting on the bench instead of a single person. Maybe someone joined a lonely person or perhaps the two people were having an argument. Both images would have very different emotional impact on the viewer. It all depends on the story you want to tell in the moment. You can draw it however you like because an artist is a creative magician! Most mundane people call it "taking creative license."

Note: I'm not trying to teach photo realism. If you want a photographic representation of a scene, then I suggest you take a proper picture with a professional camera. A photograph can be art, but art is almost never a photographic representation.

Chapter 10: Reviewing what you've learned!

Putting it all together

Start with the right **tools** for the job. Use all of your tools and a **viewfinder** to keep from getting overwhelmed by too much visual information. Create **thumbnails** to work out kinks or add them if that's your thing.

Lightly draw a **Rule of Thirds** grid on your paper to be erased later. This helps identify placement of focal points. Sketch your **Focal Point(s)** in sharp focus. Create depth by dividing your **composition** into zones. Decide whether your focal point is **Midground** or **Foreground**, add **Background** such as distant mountains, trees or clouds, which enhance the sense of space and P**erspective**, adding interest and depth to your composition. **Negative Space** is the area around the element or forms that gives the viewer's eye a place to rest so that the scene does not seem too busy. Decide if you will use **Framing** like overhanging branches or architectural things like arches, doors or a window.

Pay attention to **Value** and **Lighting**. Are you creating a high drama, **high contrast** picture or are you trying to evoke the gentle sweetness of scene in **low contrast**? Create a "**Value Translation**" to work with on your rendition of the scene by snapping a photo with your phone and removing the color. In time you will learn how those colors look as values and you won't need to take that photo.

Pay careful attention to **proportions** and the relationships between different form elements in your scene. Use comparative measurements to ensure accuracy. Use a pencil or your thumb at arm's length to measure and compare **proportions** within your scene.

Utilize natural lines, such as paths, rivers, or tree branches as **leading lines** to guide the viewer's eye through the art piece and to help create a sense of depth with the horizon, vanishing points and **perspective**.

Create **atmospheric perspective** by softening details in the background to create the illusion of depth. **Different weather conditions can drastically change the mood of a landscape.** Experiment with drawing scenes in different weather, from sunny days to stormy nights, foggy mornings or snowy evenings. If drawing bodies of water, consider how reflections can add realism and to the atmosphere of your landscape. Reflective and foggy surfaces can be challenging but rewarding to capture.

Build Narratives in your art. Whether it's a single piece or a series, storytelling adds layers of meaning and engages viewers on a deeper level. Consider the themes, ideas, emotions, and messages you want to convey and explore ways to express them visually.

Tip: Share only your best work with others and seek constructive feedback. Other perspectives can offer valuable insights and help you refine your skills. Use feedback as a tool for growth. Iterate on your work, incorporating suggestions and making improvements with each iteration.

Conclusion

Drawing nature and landscape is a celebration of the world's beauty. Through careful observation, thoughtful composition, and the application of various techniques, you can bring the serenity and majesty of the outdoors to life on paper. Let your love for life, cityscapes, or nature guide your artistic exploration and allow your drawings to become a testament to the awe-inspiring wonders that surround you wherever you are.

Above all, remember to enjoy the process of creating. Let go of perfectionism, embrace experimentation, and relish the joy that comes from expressing yourself through art. Your creative journey is a continuous exploration, and each piece is a step forward in your evolution as an artist.

Allow **your style** to evolve naturally. As you grow as an artist, your preferences and techniques may shift. Embrace this evolution as part of your wild ride. Revel in the quirks and idiosyncrasies that make your art uniquely yours.

Putting it all together is about embracing the entirety of your artistic journey, the skills you've acquired, the styles you've explored, and the stories you've told. As you synthesize these elements, your art becomes a reflection of your growth, passion, and the boundless possibilities that lie ahead. Let your creativity flow, trust in your instincts, and revel in the endless potential of your artistic expression.

Finally!

Congratulations on completing this comprehensive guide to Seeing and Drawing Like an Artist. Throughout this journey, you've explored the fundamental principles of drawing, from understanding the basics of lines and shapes to mastering composition, texture, and detail. You've ventured into the intricate realms of drawing all kinds of objects, nature, and landscapes, honing your skills and broadening your artistic horizons. Exploring different styles and capturing the essence of diverse subjects are all part of the rich tapestry that makes each artist's journey unique.

Take a moment and look at the exercises you did at the beginning. Compare that to what you can do now and let your heart swell as you see the progress you've made. Art is a lifelong journey of discovery and self-expression. As you've navigated the chapters of this guide, you've not only acquired technical skills but also gained insights into the creative process.

I hope this guide helps you to synthesize your knowledge, embrace creativity, and develop a personal style that reflects your unique artistic vision.

Remember, art is not bound by rules but is a continuous exploration of possibilities. Be an explorer.

Index of Tips

1. As you draw, try to develop a lighter hand and a loose grip to reduce stress on your bones and tendons.

2. Avoid the use of pink or other colored erasers. The colored erasers are hard erasers, and they can damage your paper.

3. Get a smaller sketch journal (5x7 or 6x9) to use for honing your skillset. Practice! Practice! Practice!

4. The only rule is: Keep your grubby hands off the paper!

5. Always use a smudge stick to create shadows or shade, not fingers.

6. Remember to use your glove or scrap paper under your hand to keep the paper clean. Get used to using ALL of your tools. Develop good habits!

7. For smoother shading with your smudge stick, scribble on scrap paper with your pencil and rub the graphite with the smudge stick. It will pick up the shading and transfer smooth shade to your drawing.

8. Lightly sketch a small sun on the paper roughly in the area of your desired light source. This is usually in the upper left or upper right corner. It helps to remember the direction of light so that you never have shadows cast at the wrong angle. When done drawing, erase the small sun.

9. Create a viewfinder to avoid overwhelming your eye. Use a scrap of paper with a square or rectangle hole cut into it. This allows you to isolate what you want to draw and disregard all the extra info in the scene.

10. Avoid placing your focal point at the exact center. The exact center is boring for the viewer. In writing, it would represent a lack of character development. Slightly off center creates visual interest and perhaps tension for the artist's story.

11. This is also a life lesson. Anything you do should <u>never</u> be an exercise in attempting perfection. Perfection is a perception of the time period, and those perceptions change. As a result, perfection can never be achieved by mere humans. You should instead focus on identifying what is important in the story of your art first, then do it. That is what makes a masterpiece.

12. The best lighting for any artwork is before 10:00am or after 2:00pm. Longer shadows are better. Shadows create interest and drama.

13. When working outside in natural light, use your phone to take a photo every 15 or 20 minutes as you work.

14. Cast shadows get shorter in the morning and longer in the evening.

15. Share only your best work with others and seek constructive feedback. Other perspectives can offer valuable insights and help you refine your skills. Use feedback as a tool for growth. Iterate on your work, incorporating suggestions and making improvements with each iteration.

Happy Drawing!

About The Author:

I always knew that I wanted to be an artist; even when a terrible high school art teacher failed me. Who fails art class? Yeah, that would be me. That teacher was about as creative as a turnip and soon after, became an administrator. She could not diminish my creativity though. She may have even sparked a bit of defiant determination.

In college we are told that getting a degree in the arts is tantamount to a life of asking, “Would you like fries with that?” I disagree. For many years after college, I followed a creative tech career path in web and software development.

However, by the early 2000s it was time for change. After the terror attack in September of 2001, I decided to pursue my true calling. I left the tech world and retreated to the mountains to pursue art full time. I’ve been managing my art business ever since and am happily following my creative passion all around the Mid-Atlantic region.

Support living artists. The dead ones don’t need it.

Made in the USA
Middletown, DE
03 January 2025

68789912R00066